EMMANUEL JOSEPH

How to Survive on Any Campus

Contents

1

Chapter 1: Campus Life 101 - An Introduction

Welcome to the exciting world of campus life! This chapter serves as your orientation to the multifaceted experience that is college or university life. Whether you're a fresh-faced freshman, a seasoned sophomore, or returning after a hiatus, understanding the fundamentals of campus life is essential for a successful journey through higher education. In this chapter, we will cover key aspects that will help you thrive during your time on any campus.

Section 1: The Campus Environment

- Subsection 1.1: Physical Layout: Get to know the layout of your campus, including academic buildings, dorms, dining halls, and recreational areas. Familiarize yourself with the campus map and learn to navigate effectively.

- Subsection 1.2: Campus Culture: Discover the unique atmosphere of your campus. Different colleges have their own cultures, traditions, and values. Understand the campus culture to better integrate and participate in the community.

Section 2: Campus Resources

 - Subsection 2.1: Academic Services: Learn about the academic resources available, such as libraries, tutoring centers, and writing labs. Find out how to utilize them to excel in your studies.

- Subsection 2.2: Student Services: Explore the various student services provided, including health and counseling centers, career services, and diversity and inclusion programs. These services are designed to support your overall well-being and personal growth.

Section 3: Campus Essentials

 - Subsection 3.1: Student ID and Campus Cards: Your student ID is your passport to campus life. It grants you access to facilities, events, and discounts. Learn how to obtain and make the most of it.

- Subsection 3.2: Safety and Security: Understand the campus safety protocols and emergency procedures. Familiarize yourself with key safety resources like campus police, emergency call boxes, and self-defense workshops.

Section 4: Time Management and Balancing Life

 - Subsection 4.1: Academic Commitments: Explore the importance of time management to handle coursework effectively. Find out how to create a study schedule and prioritize your assignments.

- Subsection 4.2: Social and Extracurricular Activities: Balance is key to a fulfilling campus life. Discover how to engage in social events and extracurricular activities while managing your academic responsibilities.

Section 5: Establishing Goals

 - Subsection 5.1: Short-term and Long-term Goals: Learn how to set and track your academic, personal, and career goals during your time on campus. Having clear goals can motivate and guide you throughout your college journey.

Section 6: Building a Support Network

- Subsection 6.1: Building Friendships: Understand the importance of creating meaningful connections and friendships. We'll explore tips on making friends and building your social network.

- Subsection 6.2: Seeking Help and Support: College life can be challenging, and it's important to know when and where to seek help. We'll discuss reaching out to professors, advisors, and counselors for support.

By the end of this chapter, you'll have a strong foundation for understanding what it takes to thrive in the dynamic environment of campus life. Whether you're just starting your journey or seeking to enhance your existing experience, the knowledge gained in this chapter will set the stage for a successful and fulfilling campus life.

2

Chapter 2: Finding Your Campus Home - Housing and Roommates

One of the most significant decisions you'll make when entering college is where you'll live on campus. Your living situation greatly influences your overall campus experience, and it's essential to find the right balance between comfort, convenience, and social connection. This chapter will guide you through the process of selecting housing and living harmoniously with roommates.

Section 1: On-Campus Housing Options
  - Subsection 1.1: Residence Halls: Discover the ins and outs of living in residence halls, including the benefits of proximity to classes and campus resources.

- Subsection 1.2: Apartments and Suites: Learn about the independent living experience in on-campus apartments and suite-style accommodations.

Section 2: Off-Campus Housing
  - Subsection 2.1: Pros and Cons: Explore the advantages and challenges of living off-campus, including budget considerations and commuting.

- Subsection 2.2: Apartment Hunting: Get valuable tips on searching for off-campus housing, including leases, budgeting, and understanding your rights as a tenant.

Section 3: Roommate Selection and Etiquette
   - Subsection 3.1: Choosing a Roommate: Discover how to find a compatible roommate, whether it's a random assignment or a friend you want to live with.

- Subsection 3.2: Roommate Communication: Learn effective communication strategies for resolving conflicts, establishing boundaries, and fostering a harmonious living environment.

Section 4: Dorm Essentials and Decorating Tips
   - Subsection 4.1: What to Bring: Get a checklist of essential items to bring to your dorm, including bedding, storage solutions, and study supplies.

- Subsection 4.2: Personalizing Your Space: Learn how to make your dorm or apartment feel like home with creative decorating ideas that express your personality.

Section 5: Safety and Security
   - Subsection 5.1: Dorm Security: Understand the importance of dorm security and learn safety measures to protect your belongings and personal well-being.

- Subsection 5.2: Fire Safety: Learn about fire safety guidelines and precautions for dorm and apartment living.

Section 6: Transitioning to Independence
   - Subsection 6.1: Managing Household Chores: Discover the responsibilities of maintaining your living space, from cleaning to grocery shopping.

- Subsection 6.2: Budgeting for Housing: Get practical financial advice for managing rent, utilities, and other living expenses.

By the end of this chapter, you'll be well-prepared to make informed decisions about your campus housing and understand how to create a comfortable and harmonious living environment. Whether you're sharing a room with roommates or living independently off-campus, this chapter will equip you with the knowledge and skills necessary to find your campus home.

3

Chapter 3: Navigating Your Campus - Maps and Directions

Navigating a college campus can be both exciting and overwhelming, especially if it's a large and complex institution. In this chapter, we'll explore strategies and resources for finding your way around campus, from deciphering maps to using technology to make your daily movements easier.

Section 1: Campus Maps and Resources
  - Subsection 1.1: Campus Map Basics: Learn how to read and interpret campus maps, including understanding building codes and landmarks.

- Subsection 1.2: Online Campus Resources: Discover the benefits of using digital resources, such as official campus websites and navigation apps, to find locations and events.

Section 2: Orientation and Campus Tours
  - Subsection 2.1: Freshman Orientation: Explore the importance of attending orientation events and getting familiar with the campus before the academic year begins.

- Subsection 2.2: Campus Tours: Learn about organized campus tours and how to make the most of them.

Section 3: Building and Room Identification
   - Subsection 3.1: Building Names and Numbers: Find out how campus buildings are named and numbered, making it easier to locate your classes and other facilities.

- Subsection 3.2: Classroom and Office Locations: Understand room numbering systems and how to efficiently find your classrooms and faculty offices.

Section 4: Transportation Options
   - Subsection 4.1: Campus Transportation Services: Explore the various transportation services offered by your campus, including shuttles, bike-sharing programs, and parking.

- Subsection 4.2: Public Transit: Learn about local public transportation options and how to navigate the public transit system.

Section 5: Navigational Tools and Technology
   - Subsection 5.1: Smartphone Apps: Discover navigation apps and other useful smartphone tools that can help you find your way around campus.

- Subsection 5.2: GPS and Wayfinding Devices: Learn about GPS devices and wayfinding technologies that can assist in campus navigation.

Section 6: Exploring Beyond Campus
   - Subsection 6.1: Nearby Off-Campus Locations: Find out how to explore the surrounding community and locate places like grocery stores, restaurants, and entertainment venues.

- Subsection 6.2: Study Spots and Hidden Gems: Discover lesser-known spots on campus that are perfect for studying or relaxing.

By the end of this chapter, you'll be equipped with the knowledge and tools to confidently navigate your college campus and the surrounding area. Whether you're a newcomer or looking to enhance your familiarity with your college's layout, this chapter will help you find your way and make the most of your time on campus.

4

Chapter 4: Budgeting 101 - Managing Your Finances

One of the most important aspects of thriving on any campus is managing your finances effectively. College life often comes with financial challenges, but with the right knowledge and strategies, you can create a budget and maintain financial stability. This chapter will provide you with the tools and tips to manage your money wisely.

Section 1: The Importance of Financial Literacy
   - Subsection 1.1: Understanding Expenses: Learn how to identify and categorize your expenses, from tuition and textbooks to personal spending.

- Subsection 1.2: Income Sources: Explore different ways to earn money while in college, including part-time jobs, internships, and financial aid.

Section 2: Creating a Budget
   - Subsection 2.1: Budgeting Basics: Understand the fundamentals of budgeting, including setting financial goals, tracking expenses, and creating a budget plan.

- Subsection 2.2: Budgeting Tools: Discover useful tools and apps for budgeting and expense tracking.

Section 3: Saving and Reducing Costs
   - Subsection 3.1: Cost-Cutting Strategies: Learn practical ways to reduce your daily expenses, from cooking at home to using student discounts.

- Subsection 3.2: Building an Emergency Fund: Understand the importance of having an emergency fund for unexpected expenses.

Section 4: Managing Debt and Student Loans
   - Subsection 4.1: Student Loans: Get an overview of student loans, their terms, and repayment options.

- Subsection 4.2: Managing Credit Cards: Learn responsible credit card use and how to build good credit.

Section 5: Scholarships and Financial Aid
   - Subsection 5.1: Scholarship Search: Explore different sources of scholarships and tips for applying successfully.

- Subsection 5.2: Financial Aid: Understand the financial aid process, including FAFSA (Free Application for Federal Student Aid) and grants.

Section 6: Financial Goals and Long-Term Planning
   - Subsection 6.1: Setting Financial Goals: Learn how to establish short-term and long-term financial goals for your college and post-graduation years.

- Subsection 6.2: Investment and Retirement Planning: Get an introduction to investment strategies and saving for your future, including retirement.

By the end of this chapter, you'll have the knowledge and tools to manage your finances effectively throughout your college journey. From creating a budget to understanding student loans and planning for the future, this chapter will help you make informed financial decisions and achieve financial stability while on any campus.

5

Chapter 5: Establishing Goals

Setting and working towards well-defined goals is an essential aspect of your college journey. In this chapter, we delve into the significance of goals, how to establish them, and the motivation they provide for your academic, personal, and career development.

Section 1: The Power of Goals

- Subsection 1.1: Understanding Goal Setting: Explore the psychology of setting goals and how they can motivate and guide you.

- Subsection 1.2: Short-term and Long-term Goals: Differentiate between short-term goals (semester or year) and long-term goals (post-graduation), and their role in your college experience.

Section 2: Academic Goals

- Subsection 2.1: GPA and Course Objectives: Understand the significance of setting academic goals like achieving a specific GPA and excelling in courses.

- Subsection 2.2: Major and Career Exploration: Learn how to set goals related to your major and career aspirations.

Section 3: Personal Development Goals

- Subsection 3.1: Health and Wellness: Explore goals related to physical and mental well-being, including fitness, stress management, and sleep habits.

- Subsection 3.2: Personal Growth: Understand how personal development goals, such as building self-confidence or improving communication skills, contribute to your college experience.

Section 4: Career and Professional Goals

- Subsection 4.1: Internships and Experience: Explore how goals related to internships, networking, and gaining professional experience can shape your career path.

- Subsection 4.2: Long-term Career Goals: Learn how to set ambitious career goals that guide your post-graduation journey.

Section 5: Goal Setting Strategies

- Subsection 5.1: Specific, Measurable, Achievable, Relevant, Time-bound (SMART) Goals: Understand the SMART criteria for setting effective goals.

- Subsection 5.2: Breaking Down Goals: Learn the importance of breaking larger goals into smaller, manageable tasks and milestones.

Section 6: Tracking and Adjusting Goals

- Subsection 6.1: Progress Monitoring: Discover strategies for tracking your progress towards goals and staying on course.

- Subsection 6.2: Adjusting Goals: Understand when and how to adapt your goals to changing circumstances and priorities.

Section 7: Staying Motivated

- Subsection 7.1: Intrinsic and Extrinsic Motivation: Explore the various sources of motivation and how to maintain enthusiasm for your goals.

- Subsection 7.2: Reward Systems: Learn how to reward yourself for achieving milestones and reaching your goals.

By the end of this chapter, you'll have the knowledge and tools to set, track, and achieve goals that will propel your college journey and prepare you for a successful future. Goal setting isn't just about dreams; it's about creating a roadmap for your college experience and beyond.

6

Chapter 6: Health and Wellness on Campus

Your well-being is a crucial part of your success and happiness during your college years. This chapter focuses on maintaining physical, mental, and emotional health while navigating the unique challenges of campus life.

Section 1: Campus Health Services
   - Subsection 1.1: Health Clinic Basics: Learn about the campus health clinic, the services it offers, and how to access medical care.

- Subsection 1.2: Mental Health Support: Explore the resources available for mental health, including counseling services, therapy, and crisis hotlines.

Section 2: Healthy Lifestyle Choices
   - Subsection 2.1: Nutrition and Eating Habits: Discover tips for maintaining a balanced diet, making healthy food choices, and budget-friendly meal planning.

- Subsection 2.2: Fitness and Exercise: Learn about fitness facilities, group classes, and ways to stay active on campus.

Section 3: Managing Stress and Wellness
   - Subsection 3.1: Stress Management: Understand strategies for dealing with academic stress, time management, and maintaining a work-life balance.

- Subsection 3.2: Sleep and Rest: Learn about the importance of quality sleep and how to establish healthy sleep habits.

Section 4: Substance Use and Abuse
   - Subsection 4.1: Alcohol and Drug Awareness: Explore the risks and consequences of alcohol and drug use, and resources for those seeking help with substance abuse.

- Subsection 4.2: Responsible Choices: Understand how to make responsible and safe choices regarding alcohol and other substances.

Section 5: Preventative Health
   - Subsection 5.1: Immunizations and Vaccinations: Learn about required and recommended vaccinations for campus life.

- Subsection 5.2: Sexual Health: Understand the importance of sexual health, safe practices, and access to resources.

Section 6: Building a Support Network
   - Subsection 6.1: Building Social Connections: Explore the importance of friendships and support networks for your overall well-being.

- Subsection 6.2: Seeking Help and Counseling: Understand how and where to seek help and counseling for various health and wellness needs.

By the end of this chapter, you'll be well-prepared to take care of your physical and mental health throughout your college journey. College can be both an exciting and challenging time, and understanding how to prioritize your well-being will ensure that you thrive in all aspects of your life while on campus.

7

Chapter 7: Getting Involved - Clubs, Organizations, and Activities

College is not just about academics; it's also an opportunity to explore your interests, passions, and hobbies. This chapter is all about finding your niche and making the most of your college experience through involvement in clubs, organizations, and various activities.

Section 1: The Benefits of Involvement
   - Subsection 1.1: Personal Growth: Explore how involvement can boost your self-confidence, leadership skills, and sense of belonging.

- Subsection 1.2: Networking Opportunities: Learn how participation in clubs and organizations can expand your social and professional network.

Section 2: Exploring Campus Clubs and Organizations
   - Subsection 2.1: Types of Groups: Discover the wide array of clubs, from academic and professional to cultural and recreational, that your campus offers.

- Subsection 2.2: Finding the Right Fit: Tips on selecting clubs and organizations that align with your interests and goals.

Section 3: Joining Clubs and Organizations
   - Subsection 3.1: Membership and Participation: Learn how to become a member and actively engage in club activities.

- Subsection 3.2: Leadership Opportunities: Understand the possibilities for taking on leadership roles within clubs and organizations.

Section 4: Campus Activities and Events
   - Subsection 4.1: Social and Recreational Activities: Explore ways to participate in campus events, including parties, sports, and cultural celebrations.

- Subsection 4.2: Volunteer Opportunities: Find out about volunteer activities and community service initiatives on campus.

Section 5: Balancing Involvement with Academics
   - Subsection 5.1: Time Management: Learn how to balance your academic commitments with your involvement in clubs and organizations.

- Subsection 5.2: Academic Benefits: Discover how participation in extracurricular activities can enhance your academic performance and career prospects.

Section 6: Making the Most of Your Involvement
   - Subsection 6.1: Building Skills: Explore the transferable skills you can gain through participation in clubs and organizations.

- Subsection 6.2: Long-Term Benefits: Understand how your involvement in college can shape your personal and professional future.

By the end of this chapter, you'll be well-equipped to navigate the world of campus clubs, organizations, and activities. Involvement can be a transformative part of your college experience, offering opportunities for personal growth, skill development, and meaningful connections with others who share your passions and interests.

8

Chapter 8: Building Strong Relationships - Friends and Support Systems

C ollege is not just about academics and personal growth; it's also a time to develop meaningful relationships. This chapter delves into the importance of building strong friendships and support networks during your college journey.

Section 1: The Significance of Social Connections
   - Subsection 1.1: Emotional Well-Being: Understand the profound impact of friendships and support systems on your mental and emotional health.

- Subsection 1.2: Academic Success: Learn how a strong support network can enhance your academic achievements.

Section 2: Making Friends and Acquaintances
   - Subsection 2.1: Orientation and Welcome Events: Explore the opportunities to meet people during freshman orientation and other introductory events.

- Subsection 2.2: Dorm and Roommate Relationships: Understand how to foster positive relationships with your roommates and dorm mates.

Section 3: Getting Involved in Campus Life
   - Subsection 3.1: Clubs and Organizations: Learn how to meet like-minded individuals by joining clubs and organizations that match your interests.

- Subsection 3.2: Volunteering and Service Activities: Discover the power of making friends through shared passions for community service.

Section 4: Effective Communication and Relationship Building
   - Subsection 4.1: Active Listening: Understand the importance of active listening in building deep and meaningful connections.

- Subsection 4.2: Conflict Resolution: Learn how to navigate conflicts within your relationships and turn them into opportunities for growth.

Section 5: Diversity and Inclusion
   - Subsection 5.1: Embracing Differences: Explore the significance of embracing diversity and inclusion on campus and how to engage with individuals from various backgrounds.

- Subsection 5.2: Cultural and Identity Groups: Discover the value of cultural and identity-based organizations and how they can be a source of connection.

Section 6: Building a Support Network
   - Subsection 6.1: Mental Health and Well-Being: Understand the role of friends and support systems in helping you maintain your mental and emotional health.

- Subsection 6.2: Academic Support: Learn how to seek academic support from peers and mentors.

By the end of this chapter, you'll have a comprehensive understanding of how to build strong relationships, make friends, and create a support network during your college experience. These connections will not only enrich your life but also provide you with a strong foundation for personal and academic success.

9

Chapter 9: Study Hacks - Strategies for Academic Success

Success in college often hinges on effective study habits and strategies. This chapter is dedicated to helping you optimize your academic performance and make the most of your learning experiences on campus.

Section 1: Study Environment and Time Management
   - Subsection 1.1: Creating a Productive Study Space: Learn how to set up an efficient and distraction-free study environment.

- Subsection 1.2: Time Management Tips: Discover techniques for managing your time effectively, including setting priorities and using study schedules.

Section 2: Note-Taking and Organization
   - Subsection 2.1: Effective Note-Taking: Explore different note-taking methods, such as the Cornell method and mind mapping.

- Subsection 2.2: Organization and Filing: Understand the importance of organizing your notes, materials, and assignments.

Section 3: Study Techniques and Learning Styles
   - Subsection 3.1: Active Learning: Learn about active learning strategies, including problem-solving, group discussions, and interactive studying.

- Subsection 3.2: Tailoring to Your Learning Style: Discover how to adapt your study techniques to your unique learning style, whether you're a visual, auditory, or kinesthetic learner.

Section 4: Research and Resources
   - Subsection 4.1: Library Skills: Explore effective library research, citation methods, and finding scholarly sources.

- Subsection 4.2: Online Resources: Learn how to make the most of online resources, including digital libraries and academic databases.

Section 5: Test Preparation and Performance
   - Subsection 5.1: Test-Taking Strategies: Discover techniques for preparing and performing well on exams, including managing test anxiety and time.

- Subsection 5.2: Essay Writing and Research Papers: Get tips on effective essay writing, research, and structuring academic papers.

Section 6: Seeking Help and Academic Support
   - Subsection 6.1: Faculty Interaction: Understand the importance of building relationships with professors and seeking help when needed.

- Subsection 6.2: Tutoring and Academic Support Centers: Learn about available resources, including tutoring services and academic support centers.

Section 7: Balancing Academics with Extracurriculars
   - Subsection 7.1: Time Management: Explore strategies for maintaining a balance between your academic commitments and involvement in clubs and organizations.

- Subsection 7.2: Staying Healthy: Discover the connection between academic performance and physical and mental health.

By the end of this chapter, you'll be well-prepared to excel academically in college by implementing effective study habits and strategies. These skills will not only help you succeed in your coursework but also enhance your overall learning experience on campus.

10

Chapter 10: Staying Safe on Campus

Safety is a top priority on any college campus. This chapter is dedicated to helping you understand the measures and precautions you can take to ensure your well-being and security while pursuing your education.

Section 1: Campus Safety Protocols

- Subsection 1.1: Emergency Procedures: Learn about the campus's emergency protocols, including what to do in the event of fire, severe weather, or other emergencies.

- Subsection 1.2: Safety Apps and Resources: Discover safety apps and online resources that can help you stay informed and connected during emergencies.

Section 2: Personal Safety

- Subsection 2.1: Self-Defense and Safety Workshops: Explore the benefits of self-defense training and personal safety workshops offered on campus.

- Subsection 2.2: Nighttime Safety: Learn strategies for staying safe during nighttime activities, such as walking alone on campus.

Section 3: Residence Safety

- Subsection 3.1: Dorm and Apartment Security: Understand the importance of securing your living space, including locking doors and windows.

- Subsection 3.2: Fire Safety: Learn about fire safety precautions and the proper use of fire safety equipment in your residence.

Section 4: Transportation and Commuting Safety
- Subsection 4.1: Campus Shuttles and Public Transit: Discover safety measures and tips for using campus shuttles and public transportation.

- Subsection 4.2: Bicycle and Pedestrian Safety: Understand how to stay safe while walking or cycling on and around campus.

Section 5: Health and Well-Being
- Subsection 5.1: Mental Health Resources: Learn about the importance of mental health support and where to access counseling and therapy services.

- Subsection 5.2: Sexual Assault Prevention and Support: Explore resources related to sexual assault prevention, awareness, and support services.

Section 6: Building a Safe Community
- Subsection 6.1: Reporting Incidents: Understand the importance of reporting incidents or concerns to campus authorities and how to do so.

- Subsection 6.2: Community Involvement: Learn how to actively contribute to a safe and respectful campus environment.

By the end of this chapter, you'll have the knowledge and tools to prioritize your safety and well-being on campus. College is a place for growth, learning, and exploration, and feeling safe is essential for you to fully engage with your educational experience.

11

Chapter 11: Career and Future Planning

While college is a time of learning and personal growth, it's also an opportunity to prepare for your future career. This chapter focuses on the steps you can take to plan and work towards a successful career path.

Section 1: Exploring Career Paths

- Subsection 1.1: Self-Assessment: Discover how to assess your skills, interests, and values to help you identify potential career paths.

- Subsection 1.2: Career Counseling: Learn about the benefits of career counseling services offered on campus.

Section 2: Building a Strong Resume and Portfolio

- Subsection 2.1: Resume Writing: Get tips on crafting an effective resume that highlights your qualifications and experiences.

- Subsection 2.2: Portfolios and Online Presence: Understand the importance of an online presence and how to build a professional portfolio.

Section 3: Networking and Internships

- Subsection 3.1: Networking Strategies: Explore how to build professional connections with professors, alumni, and industry professionals.

- Subsection 3.2: Internship Opportunities: Learn how to secure internships and gain valuable work experience in your chosen field.

Section 4: Job Search and Interview Skills
   - Subsection 4.1: Job Search Techniques: Discover how to search for job opportunities, both on and off campus.

- Subsection 4.2: Interview Preparation: Get tips on preparing for job interviews, including practice questions and strategies.

Section 5: Graduate School and Advanced Degrees
   - Subsection 5.1: Considering Graduate School: Explore the decision-making process for pursuing advanced degrees and the application process.

- Subsection 5.2: Financial Planning: Understand how to plan for the financial costs of graduate school and the availability of financial aid.

Section 6: Long-Term Career Planning
   - Subsection 6.1: Setting Career Goals: Learn how to set short-term and long-term career goals.

- Subsection 6.2: Life After Graduation: Discover strategies for transitioning to the workforce or advanced education upon graduation.

By the end of this chapter, you'll be well-equipped to plan for your future career and take the necessary steps to reach your professional goals. College is a crucial time for building the foundation of your career, and the knowledge and skills you gain during your academic journey will play a pivotal role in your future success.

Chapter 12: Thriving Beyond Campus - Preparing for Life After Graduation

Your college years prepare you for a successful transition into the world beyond campus. This chapter explores how to make the most of your college experience, set goals for your future, and prepare for life after graduation.

Section 1: Reflecting on Your College Experience
  - Subsection 1.1: Identifying Achievements: Reflect on your accomplishments, skills gained, and personal growth during your college journey.

- Subsection 1.2: Lessons Learned: Understand the valuable life lessons and experiences you've had on campus.

Section 2: Setting Post-Graduation Goals
  - Subsection 2.1: Career Goals: Define your short-term and long-term career objectives and create a plan to achieve them.

- Subsection 2.2: Personal Goals: Set personal goals for your future, including relationships, health, and lifestyle.

Section 3: Transitioning to the Workforce
   - Subsection 3.1: Job Search and Applications: Learn about strategies for finding job opportunities and preparing strong applications.

- Subsection 3.2: Interview Skills: Understand how to excel in job interviews and leave a lasting impression on potential employers.

Section 4: Financial Planning and Budgeting
   - Subsection 4.1: Financial Independence: Prepare for managing your finances independently after graduation.

- Subsection 4.2: Loan Repayment: Learn about student loan repayment options and how to create a manageable financial plan.

Section 5: Building a Support Network
   - Subsection 5.1: Professional Connections: Expand your network by connecting with alumni and professionals in your field.

- Subsection 5.2: Mentoring Relationships: Seek out mentors who can offer guidance and support as you transition into your career.

Section 6: Life After College
   - Subsection 6.1: Adjusting to the Real World: Understand the challenges and opportunities that come with post-graduation life.

- Subsection 6.2: Continuing Education and Professional Development: Explore options for ongoing education and skill development to advance your career.

By the end of this chapter, you'll be well-prepared to thrive in the world beyond campus. Your college experience has equipped you with knowledge, skills, and a network of contacts that will be invaluable as you take your next steps into the professional world.